Fairy Tale Frolic

Interdisciplinary Units and Enrichment Activities

by Sue Wright

Incentive Publications, Inc.
Nashville, Tennessee

Cover and illustrations by Dianna Meadows
Edited by Leslie Britt and Cherrie Farnette

ISBN 0-86530-260-X

PRINTED IN THE UNITED STATES OF AMERICA

Table of Contents

*"He that has found a way to keep a child's spirit easy, active, and free,
and yet at the same time to restrain him from many things he has
a mind to, and to draw him to things that are uneasy to him,
has in my opinion, got the true secret of education."*

— John Locke

DID YOUR LAST LETTER TO SANTA READ LIKE THIS?

Dear Santa,
Please send me a thematic unit my primary students would enjoy. I need one that promotes thinking skills and is based on whole language educational theory. Help!
Yours truly,
A. Harried Teacher

If Santa did not bring you such a unit this year, there is still hope. Try the units in this book based on a theme youngsters love—fairy tales. Seven fairy tales comprise the core of these units: *Snow White, Cinderella, Rapunzel, Beauty and the Beast, The Little Mermaid, The Princess and the Pea,* and *Sleeping Beauty.* The format is designed to allow teachers working in teams to share the units. Teams may choose to combine their culminating activities into a fairy tale "expo." For those teachers working alone, any number of story units can be used to complete the study. The levels of Bloom's Taxonomy and Williams' Primary Mental Abilities of Human Intellect are noted next to activities as applicable.

KEY TO TERMS:

Bloom
- **(K)** Knowledge
- **(C)** Comprehension
- **(AP)** Application
- **(AN)** Analysis
- **(S)** Synthesis
- **(E)** Evaluation

Williams
- **(FL)** Fluency
- **(FX)** Flexibility
- **(O)** Originality
- **(EL)** Elaboration

THEMATIC FOCUS:

To assist primary students in the development of language arts, math, science, social studies, and thinking skills through the study of fairy tales

OBJECTIVES:
Thinking Skills
- To develop thinking skills based on the levels of Bloom's Taxonomy
- To enhance divergent thinking skills
- To develop creative writing skills
- To encourage creative thinking

Mathematics Skills

- To provide practice solving word problems
- To learn how to set up bar graphs
- To develop estimation skills
- To practice basic multiplication facts
- To practice measurement skills using inches, feet, yards, pints, and quarts
- To practice basic addition facts
- To practice the associative property in multiplication

Language Arts Skills

- To practice identifying main ideas in paragraphs
- To increase skills in writing couplets
- To increase spelling ability
- To practice Dolch sight words vocabulary
- To increase skills in sentence construction
- To develop skills in changing statements into questions
- To practice correct verb usage
- To practice consonant and initial consonant identification and blend identification
- To identify compound words
- To practice identifying root words
- To practice identifying vowel sounds
- To practice identifying parts of speech: nouns, verbs, and adjectives

Social Studies Skills

- To discover how other peoples have lived throughout different time periods and in different environments
- To develop mapping skills
- To discover the location of rain forests and learn about their plant, animal, and human habitats
- To identify five major physical features on the United States map
- To learn about the travels of Johnny Appleseed

Science Skills

- To learn stages of plant growth and factors affecting plant growth through the process of experimentation
- To define weather
- To develop an understanding of what causes rain, snow, sleet, hail, tornadoes, and hurricanes
- To discover how an anemometer and rain gauge work by building models
- To learn varieties of apples
- To name different varieties of leaves
- To develop hypothesizing skills
- To develop an understanding of the basic food groups and balanced meals
- To discover facts about the ocean

Cinderella

Cinderella

Introductory Activities

1. Introduce the unit by viewing the movie version of the Cinderella story. After viewing the movie, discuss the plot with the class. **(K) (C)**

2. Read *Cinderella*. Discuss with the class the story's plot, pointing out similarities and differences between the book version and the movie version. **(K) (C)**

3. Ask the students to compare and contrast the movie version of the Cinderella story with the book version. Introduce brainstorming and chart the students' responses on the chalkboard. **(C) (AN)**

4. Ask each student to evaluate the version he or she prefers and to write a sentence or two explaining reasons for his or her preference. **(E) (FL) (FX) (O) (EL) (S)**

Brainstormers

WHAT IF...?

1. What if there were no pumpkins in the garden? How might Cinderella have arrived at the ball?

2. What other kinds of animals would have made good horses for the coach? What other kinds of animals would have made a good footman?

3. What if the garden had been bare of animals? How would the fairy godmother have handled this problem?

4. What if the Prince had not found Cinderella's shoe?

5. What if Cinderella had not lost her shoe?

6. What if the Prince had stepped on the glass slipper and broke it?

(K) (C) (AP) (S) (FL) (FX) (O) (EL)

Subject Integration

SPELLING & VOCABULARY

SAMPLE VOCABULARY WORDS: *Cinderella, sisters, king, prince, ball, gown, pumpkin, mice, coach, rags, horse, glass, shoes, marry, clock, girl, palace, two, love, garden, mother, father*

Cinderella

English

NAME THAT NOUN

Make flash cards using vocabulary words from the *Cinderella* Unit. Include all parts of speech: nouns, verbs, adjectives, adverbs, etc. To play the game, divide the class into two teams. Give each team a set of twenty cards. The team to first find all of its noun (or adjective, adverb, verb, etc.) cards wins the game. **(K) (C)**

NOUN BEE

Conduct the noun bee as you would a spelling bee, with the exception that each student must decide whether or not a word is a noun. You may hold an adjective bee, a verb bee, or an adverb bee, as well. **(K) (C)**

Creative Writing

CINDERELLA BOOKS

(These ideas can be used for role play activities. Students who are unable to write can tape record their endings for sharing.)

Divide the class into three groups, and ask each group to write a section of the Cinderella story in their own words (either the beginning, middle, or ending of the story). The group chosen to complete the story's conclusion should change the ending in some way. As a class, proof, rewrite, and "publish" this new version of the Cinderella story.

VARIATIONS:

1. Divide the class into four groups, each responsible for producing its own version of the book.
2. Ask the class to illustrate a picture book of the Cinderella story. Each illustration should be accompanied by a caption.
3. Share your books with other primary classrooms by:
   • having a "book tour" and reading your stories to other classes
   • inviting other classes to your room for the sharing of the stories

(AP) (S) (FX) (O)

Cinderella

Reading

Cut apart sections of the Cinderella story and glue them onto 5" x 7" index cards. Let each student select one passage to read aloud. Each student should also tell the part of the story that comes before and after his or her excerpt.

MAGIC CONSONANTS

Give each student a square of white typing paper on which you have printed a large consonant letter using a white crayon. Have each student color the page with a magic marker. When students have discovered their letters, assign them to locate words in *Cinderella* which begin with their letters and read them aloud. **(K) (C) (AN)**

Math

Choose a set of word problems from a math textbook or workbook and rewrite them with a Cinderella theme. Examples:

1. Cinderella worked 8 hours on Monday and 3 hours on Tuesday. How many more hours did she work on Monday than on Tuesday?

2. Cinderella went to the garden and picked 4 tomatoes, 8 carrots, 5 onions, and 6 squash. How many vegetables did she pick?

3. On Friday, Cinderella's stepsisters spent 3 hours dressing and putting on their make-up. They spent twice as much time dressing and putting on make-up on Saturday. How long did it take them to dress and put on their make-up on Saturday?

4. Cinderella polished silver all day. She shined 24 forks, 24 knives, and 30 spoons. How much silverware did she shine?

(AN) (AP)

Graphing

Teach a lesson on bar graphs. Ask the class to construct a bar graph of the heights of *Cinderella* characters using the following information:

Cinderella is 5' 2"   The Prince is 5' 9"
Her stepmother is 5'   The fairy godmother is 4' 8"
The oldest stepsister is 5' 3"

(C) (AN)

A reproducible math activity worksheet is included in this unit (page 18)

Science

A STUDY OF PUMPKINS

GROWTH STAGES OF A PUMPKIN

1. Sprout pumpkin seeds in glass jars. Dampen paper towels and wrap one around the inside of each glass jar. Fill each jar with enough water to keep the towel wet. Place pumpkin seeds between the towel and the inside of the jar so that they can receive moisture and still be viewed.

2. Plant sprouts in paper cups of dirt and watch them grow.

3. Have the class draw the growth stages of a pumpkin from seed to plant. **(K) (C) (AP)**

4. Graph the growth of a selected number of plants. **(C) (AN)**

Just watch me grow!

EXPERIMENT—WHAT DOES A PLANT NEED TO GROW?

Subject a grown plant to variables such as no water, too much water, no light, constant light, no fertilizer, too much fertilizer, etc. Select another plant to act as the control plant. This plant should be given adequate water, light, and fertilizer. Select a third plant to receive no care at all. Evaluate the growth of all plants, and have the class surmise the elements needed for a plant to grow. **(AP) (AN) (E)**

Character Match Game

Make three sets of cards: names of the characters in Cinderella, the characters' pictures, and the characters' characteristics. Students match the name cards with their pictures and characteristics.

Match cards are provided on pages 16–17. Four boxes have been left blank for you to write in your own characteristics. Answer key is on page 95. **(AP) (AN)**

ocial Studies

Examine maps, paying special attention to map keys and directional markers. Discuss with students the importance and use of these map tools. Discuss the type of town in which Cinderella might have lived. Assign pairs of students to draw a city map for Cinderella in the event that she becomes lost on the way home from the palace. Each map should include a map key and major city buildings. **(AP) (S) (FL) (O) (EL)**

rt

Make papier mâché pumpkins. Have the students paint Halloween faces on their pumpkins and decorate them with yarn, glitter, sequins, buttons, colored macaroni, etc. **(EL) (FL) (O)**

usic

"Three Little Pumpkins"
Sing these new lyrics to the familiar tune of "Three Blind Mice."

Three little pumpkins, three little pumpkins,
Sitting on a fence, sitting on a fence.
They want to go to the Prince's ball,
And dance until the break of dawn,
But Mother said, "You're all too young."
Poor little pumpkins. Poor little pumpkins!

Cinderella

Planning for Gifted Learners

Two reproducible logical elimination brainteasers are provided on pages 20 and 21. For those students who have never completed an elimination puzzle, a third puzzle entitled "Chore Time" is provided on page 19 as a teaching tool.

Teach students to solve logical elimination puzzles by using a grid, marking it with O's for the correct answers and X's for the answers they are eliminating.

EXAMPLE: (AN) (S) (E) (FL)

	YELLOW	WHITE	ORANGE	RED
Carrots	X	X	O	X
Corn	O	X	X	X
Tomato	X	X	X	O
Onion	X	O	X	X

Culminating Activity

TASTING PARTY AND PLAY

Call upon parent volunteers to help you plan a tasting party. Serve pumpkin pie, pumpkin bread, pumpkin cake, pumpkin cookies, and roasted pumpkin seeds. Invite parents to join you and have students work on a display. For entertainment, let the students perform the *Cinderella* story with their favorite new ending.

Cinderella

Stepmother	Fairy Godmother	Cinderella	Stepsisters
Prince	Old	Greedy	Ugly
Cruel	Favored her own daughters	Kind	Helpful
Knows magic	Generous	Sweet	Loving
Young	Pretty	Hard-working	Uncomplaining

Cheerful	Lazy	Jealous	Mean
Spoiled	King's son	Honorable	Handsome
In love with Cinderella	Looking for a wife	Rich	

Pumpkin Quest

1. Cinderella ironed 4 dresses for her stepsisters on Monday, 3 on Tuesday, and 5 on Wednesday. How many dresses did she iron on those 3 days?_____

2. Cinderella made vegetable soup for supper on Friday. She used 4 tomatoes, 3 carrots, 1 onion, and 2 cabbages. How many vegetables did she use in all?_____

3. Cinderella swept 2 rooms in the house and dusted twice as many rooms as she swept. How many rooms did she clean?_____

4. The stepsisters went shopping for new spring hats. The older sister bought 11 hats, and the younger sister bought 3. How many more hats did the older sister buy than did the younger sister? _____

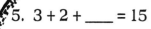

5. $3 + 2 + \underline{\hspace{1cm}} = 15$
6. $11 - 5 = \underline{\hspace{1cm}}$
7. $16 - 8 = \underline{\hspace{1cm}}$

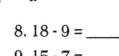

8. $18 - 9 = \underline{\hspace{1cm}}$
9. $15 - 7 = \underline{\hspace{1cm}}$
10. $12 - 6 = \underline{\hspace{1cm}}$

11. $14 - 5 = \underline{\hspace{1cm}}$
12. $17 - 9 = \underline{\hspace{1cm}}$

Name _____

Chore Time

The mean stepsisters have been playing tricks on Cinderella by hiding her mop, bucket, broom, and dust rags. The places she must look for them are the garden, her stepmother's bedroom, the barn, and the backyard. Help her find her cleaning tools quickly by matching them to the places where they are hidden. Use the clues below. Mark your answers on the grid by using an O for each correct answer and an X for each incorrect answer.

CLUES

1. Cinderella followed a trail of water and found her bucket in her stepmother's bedroom.
2. While she was milking, Cinderella found the mop.
3. Cinderella was picking tomatoes when she saw her dust rags.

	GARDEN	BEDROOM	BARN	BACKYARD
Mop				
Bucket				
Broom				
Dust rags				

Name _____

Meet the Prince

When Cinderella arrived at the palace ball, there were four young ladies standing in line to meet the Prince. Their names were Mary, Janet, Elizabeth, and Anna. Using the clues provided below, find out who was standing first, second, third, and last in line.

CLUES
1. Elizabeth was behind everyone.
2. Anna was between Mary and Elizabeth

HINT: This puzzle can be solved without a grid.

Name _____

The Ball Gown Mystery

Throughout the Prince's ball, Mary, Janet, Elizabeth, and Anna fought over which one would be able to dance with the Prince the most. Each thought she had the best chance to dance with the Prince because of her lovely ball gown. The colors of their gowns were red, blue, green, and pink. Match the colors of the ball gowns to the girls.

CLUES

1. Elizabeth hated the color pink and also refused to wear a gown the same color as her hair.
2. Mary, the youngest of the four, wore blue.
3. Janet wore a red ball gown to the ball last year and refused to be seen in the same color this year. She wanted her gown to match her eyes.

	BLUE	PINK	RED	GREEN
Mary				
Janet				
Elizabeth				
Anna				

Name _____

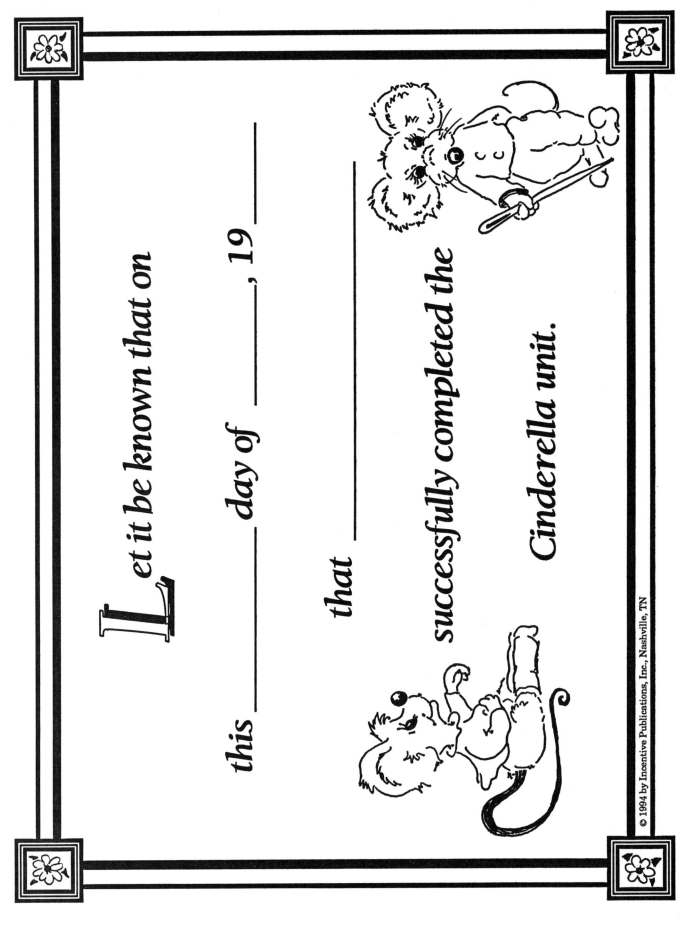

Let it be known that on

this _____ day of _____, 19____

that _____

successfully completed the

Cinderella unit.

The Princess and the Pea

The Princess and the Pea

Introductory Activities

1. Introduce *The Princess and the Pea* by keeping its title a secret while you play this game. Place a dried pea in a box and tape the lid to the box so that it will not come off. Let the students shake the box and ask questions which will help them discover the item in the box. (Sample questions: "Is the item large?" "Is it larger than a tennis ball?" "Has it ever been alive?") All questions which are asked must be answerable with a "yes" or "no." Do not allow the students to make a guess until a question is asked. **(FL) (FX) (AN)**

2. Read aloud *The Princess and the Pea*. Discuss with the students the fairy tale's plot to assess the students' comprehension. Make stick puppets and dramatize the story. **(K) (C) (AP) (O) (EL) (FL) (FX)**

3. Ask someone to dress like a princess and visit your classroom to tell the fairy tale in her own words, using first person point of view.

Brainstormers

WHAT IF...?

1. What if the Queen had decided to test the princess by putting an object as big as an orange under her mattress?

2. What could the Queen have put under the mattress that would have worked as well as the pea?

3. What if the Princess had refused to marry the Prince? How could he have won her heart?

4. If it had not been storming that night, what else could have happened to bring the Princess to the castle door?

5. What if the Queen had wanted to test the Princess a second time? What could she have done?

(K) (C) (AP) (S) (FL) (FX) (O) (EL)

Subject Integration

SPELLING & VOCABULARY

SAMPLE VOCABULARY WORDS: *prince, princess, pea, real, kingdom, storm, thunder, king, queen, guest, sleep, mattress, lump, black, blue, twenty*

Reading

BEAN BAG TOSS

Materials Needed: • small bean bag • two pieces of posterboard • a yard stick
• 5" x 7" cards • a marker

Divide each poster into eight equally-sized squares. Write a number between one and five at the bottom of each square and tape the posters together. Label each 5" x 7" card with Dolch sight words and tape one per square. Divide the class into teams. Mark a line on the floor with masking tape to indicate where the players will stand. Each student pitches the bean bag at a square. If the student can pronounce the word on the card on which his or her bag lands, his or her team receives those points. The first team to earn 50 points wins the game.

Change the cards as a word is pronounced correctly. You may wish to include on the game board some penalty squares such as "Lose Your Turn," "Lose One Point," etc.

EGG CARTON TOSS

Materials Needed: • egg carton • permanent ink marker
• marble • Dolch cards from previous game

Cut the lid from a sturdy egg carton or use an old egg tray from your refrigerator. Randomly mark numbers from one to six in the bottom of each egg cup. Divide the class into teams and play the game by tossing the marble into the egg carton. Follow the rules of the Bean Bag Toss game, above.

SILENT E POWER

Make matching puzzle pieces from tagboard, using word pairs which change their vowel sounds from short to long when the silent E is present. Have them match the pairs and then pronounce the words to their partners. Sample Word List: *kit, kite; tub, tube; bit, bite; sit, site; pin, pine; fin, fine; hat, hate; hop, hope; cub, cube; tap, tape; not, note; cap, cape; rid, ride; pan, pane; din, dine; gal, gale; cut, cute; rob, robe; mop, mope*

NAME THAT WORD

Cut out pictures from magazines and catalogs. Select pictures which have objects that can be named by their beginning consonants. Mount pictures on cards and laminate. Use as flash cards to drill initial consonant sounds. (K) (C) (AP) (AN)

The Princess and the Pea

Creative Writing

1. Each student chooses one of the "What If . . .?" exercises from the Brainstormers section (page 24) and writes a new version of *The Princess and the Pea*.

2. Story Starter:
   "Once upon a time there was a beautiful princess who would eat nothing but green peas . . ."

3. Introducing Couplets:
   Introduce the students to writing poetry by teaching them to compose couplets.
   Explain that a couplet is a two-line poem that states one idea. These two lines may or may not rhyme. Example:

   > *My new shoes are quite neat.*
   > *They shine so bright on my feet.*

   Ask the students to identify the idea expressed in this couplet.
   Then examine these couplets from Old Mother Goose nursery rhymes.

   > *"Christmas comes but once a year,*
   > *And when it comes it brings good cheer."*

   > *"Jerry Hall, he was so small,*
   > *A rat could eat him, hat and all."*

   > *"Rain, rain, go to Spain*
   > *And never come back again."*

   Ask students to compose couplets of their own.

4. Introducing Rhythm:
   Have the class say the above rhymes aloud. As they read them, clap out the rhythm.
   Ask: *"Do you hear any special beat as you say the words 'Jerry Hall, he was so small'* or *'A rat could eat him, hat and all'? What kind of beat do you feel?"*

   Have the class clap out the rhythm as you read aloud the other couplets.

   Brainstorm with the class to finish these lines and create class couplets, concentrating on keeping the rhythm consistent. **(AP) (S) (FL) (FX) (O) (EL)**

   a. My hair is frizzy as a mop...

   b. The dog is such a wonderful pet...

   c. My cat will act a little funny...

   d. Soup for supper is just dandy...

The Princess and the Pea

English

ADJECTIVE DRILL

Collect a random selection of objects and place them in an opaque plastic bag. Let students reach into the bag and select objects to show the class. Brainstorm for words which describe each object. List the adjectives on the board as they are named. When all objects have been examined, assign each student to write one sentence about each object, using some of the adjectives which have been named. **(K) (C)**

Drama

CHORAL READING OF "THE POOR PRINCESS"

Solo One:	Once there was a prince who wanted a wife.
Solo Two:	He vowed to have a true princess to share his life.
Solo One:	He looked around the world only to find
Solo Three:	That no one was as good as the girl in his mind.
Solo One:	Then one night in rain and lightning galore
Solo Four:	A princess, wet and cold, knocked at his door.
Solo One:	The queen had a plan to put the princess to the test.
Solo Five:	She stacked twenty mattresses and invited her to rest.
Solo One:	But before she sat down, the queen placed a pea
Solo Six:	Beneath her mattresses and said, "We'll see."
Solo One:	The princess tossed and turned until the break of day.
Solo Seven:	When the queen asked her if she slept, she said, "No way!"
Solo Seven:	"I'm black and blue all over from a lump in my bed.
	If I sleep here another night, I'm sure I'll be dead."
Solo One:	So the moral of this sad story is:
All:	When traveling, always carry your own sleeping bag!

The Princess and the Pea

Math

ESTIMATION AND MEASUREMENT

Fill a quart jar with dried peas. Let students guess how many peas are in the jars by placing their guesses on a slip of paper and dropping them in a box. Offer a prize for the person whose guess is the closest to the correct number. After the peas are counted and the winner is determined, use the peas to make a measurement comparison between a quart jar and two pint jars.

A YARD OF PEAS

To practice measuring with a ruler and yard stick, line up peas and judge the number of peas required to make a foot, two feet, and one yard. Let the students estimate the answers before you measure.

MULTIPLYING PEAS

Teach the two's multiplication table by using peas to visually represent each multiplication fact. (K) (C) (AP)

Graphing

Bring in four to five seeds of different sizes. Help the students identify each type of seed. Line up each type of seed alongside a ruler to see how many seeds it takes to make a foot. Assign the class to graph the results of their experiment.

VARIATION: SEED POSTER

Assign younger students to make seed posters. Give each student several different types of seeds and have them arrange each set into an illustration of a simple addition problem. Then have them glue the seeds to the poster and write the math fact represented by each seed group. (K) (C) (AP) (AN)

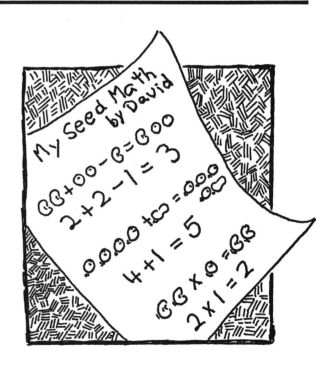

The Princess and the Pea

Science

RESEARCH

Brainstorm for weather-related questions the students would like answered.

Examples: *"What makes it rain?" "What makes it snow?" "What makes it hail or sleet?" "What causes thunder and lightning?" "What causes a tornado?" "What is the difference between a tornado and a hurricane?"*

Assign two-member research teams to investigate a question of their choice. Have them present their findings in a poster, booklet, pamphlet, skit, filmstrip, scroll, diorama and short report, or flipbook format. **(K) (C) (AP) (S) (FL) (O) (EL)**

WHAT IS WEATHER?

Weather includes all of the daily changes in temperature, wind, moisture, and air pressure. Of all the forces of nature, weather most consistently influences everyone's lives. It can make us feel cold or warm, happy or unhappy. It affects crops, our daily work, sports events, food prices, transportation, communication, shoppers' habits, and our global environment. Brainstorm with the students to name specific ways weather affects our lives.

Have students students share their feelings about the weather.

1. On cold days I feel...
2. On hot days I feel...
3. On snowy days I feel...
4. On rainy days I feel...
5. On sunny days I feel...

THE WEATHER MAP

Ask different students to bring in the weather map from the newspaper each day for a week. Using a wall map of your region or the entire country, mark the weather patterns which are shown in the newspaper. *(Patterns for the symbols are found on page 36.)* On your daily calendar, mark the actual weather you are having and compare it to the newspaper's predictions. Some students might like to keep a weather journal, as well.

WEATHER INSTRUMENTS

Introduce weather instruments to the students:

- thermometers (Fahrenheit/Celsius) to measure temperature
- barometers (aneroid/mercurial) to measure air pressure
- rain gauge to measure precipitation
- anemometer and weather vane to measure wind speed and direction
- weather balloons, weather satellites, RADAR

The Princess and the Pea

S cience

MAKING WEATHER INSTRUMENTS

1. Rain Gauge
   Materials Needed:
   - medium-size clear glass jar
   - funnel with a diameter twice the diameter of the jar
   - 6" clear plastic ruler

   Place the funnel inside the jar, making sure its diameter is twice that of the jar's diameter. Attach the ruler to the outside of the jar with clear tape. At the first sign of rain, place the gauge outside in a level area removed from trees and buildings so that it will receive rainfall. Retrieve the gauge as soon as possible after the rain so that evaporation will not affect your measurement. Remember, since you used a funnel to collect additional rain, the amount measured is not the actual inches of rainfall. If the funnel has a diameter twice the diameter of the jar, the actual inches of rainfall will be one-fourth of the measured amount.

2. Anemometer
   Materials Needed:
   - lightweight sticks, approximately 12" long
   - hot glue, string, or electrical tape
   - 4 plastic cups
   - pole, approximately 24" long
   - 4 tacks
   - nail and several washers

   To make a cup anemometer, construct a crossbeam from the 2 lightweight sticks, either using the hot glue, wrapping the sticks with the string or tape, or using the cutting/overlapping method. Attach the four cups to the arms as shown in the illustration so that the cups will catch the wind. Attach the crossbeam to the pole with the nail, using enough washers to make the crossbeam turn freely. Place the unit where it can catch the wind and count the number of turns it makes in 30 seconds. Divide that number by five to calculate the wind speed in miles per hour. **(K) (C) (AP) (AN) (E)**

30

The Princess and the Pea

Social Studies

THE RAIN FOREST

1. Locate on maps and globes the world's rain forest areas. Introduce the term equator and explain to students why these regions have tropical rain forest climates.

2. Brainstormers:
   - Ask students to guess the types of plants that live in a typical rain forest.
   - Ask students to guess the types of animals that live in a typical rain forest.
   - Ask the students to brainstorm what it would be like to live in a tropical climate (types of homes, food, clothing, lifestyles, etc.)

   Record students' answers on a chart so that when this study is completed, they can evaluate the accuracy of their estimations.

3. Assign two-member teams to research information on tropical plants, tropical animals, human habitats in the tropics, and human lifestyles in the tropics. Require that the research teams present their information to the class in some sort of visual display (murals, poster-size books, etc.)

4. Locate materials about the disappearance of the world's rain forests and share them with the class, emphasizing the wise use of our natural resources.

5. Bring to class tropical fruits for the students to sample.

(K) (C) (AP) (AN) (E) (FL) (FX) (EL) (O)

Art

COUPLET MURAL

Students write couplets (see Creative Writing section, page 26) on bulletin board paper and illustrate them.

MOSAICS

Color dried peas different colors and distribute them to students who make patterns or pictures by gluing the peas on pieces of posterboard.

(EL) (FL) (O)

The Princess and the Pea

Planning for Gifted Learners

One logical elimination puzzle and a brainteaser are included in this section. (See pages 33 and 34 for the worksheets.) **(AN) (S) (E) (FL)**

Culminating Activity

CLASSROOM CARNIVAL

Set up carnival booths in the classroom and invite parents to join the fun. Ask for parent volunteers to provide cookies, candy, brownies, and other treats cooked as "tropical food"— containing coconut, dates, figs, and nuts. Use these treats as booth prizes. Give each student a certain number of booth tickets (pattern on page 37) to spend at the carnival.

BOOTHS 1–2:
Display the projects which the students have completed.

BOOTH 3 "TROPICAL DELIGHTS":
Serve pineapple juice and tropical punch.

BOOTH 4 "FISH POND":
Attach paper clips to the string on a fishing pole. Each fisherman will catch a fish containing a question. (The question should be related to your current social studies or science unit. See pattern on page 37).

BOOTH 5 "DUCK POND":
Float plastic ducks in a tub of water. Mark each duck with a number. Keep a corresponding numbered list of questions from *The Princess and the Pea* and the science or social studies units to ask to each student as he or she picks up a duck. Divide the list into easy and difficult questions to meet the different needs of the students.

BOOTH 6 "BOWLING":
Use empty soda pop bottles (one liter) as the pins and a rubber ball. Give each participant three chances to knock down all of the bottles.

BOOTH 7 "BASKETBALL TOSS":
Set up a small toy hoop that attaches to a wall with a suction cup. Each participant has three chances to score.

BOOTH 8 "TENNIS BALL TOSS":
Participants toss a tennis ball into a bucket. Give each participant three chances to score.

A Prickly Princess Puzzle

The queen wants to test you just like she tested the princess in the fairy tale. She has made the hardest puzzle she can for you to solve. If you can solve this puzzle, you can live in the castle with the royal family.

1. Change one letter in each row to spell a new word. The last word in each set is given to you. Example: <u>SAT</u> is changed to <u>SET</u> which is changed to <u>BET</u> which becomes <u>BEG</u>. Remember, you can change only one letter at a time.

    BED   ____ ____   FED
    RAIN   ____ ____ ____   BOIL
    PEA   ____ ____ ____   FEE
    BLUE   ____ ____   FLEE

2. Can you think of 8 four-letter words that end in -OLD?

    _____   _____
    _____   _____
    _____   _____
    _____   _____

3. Can you think of 7 four-letter words ending in -UMP?

    _____   _____
    _____   _____
    _____   _____
    _____

Name _____

The Mattress Puzzle

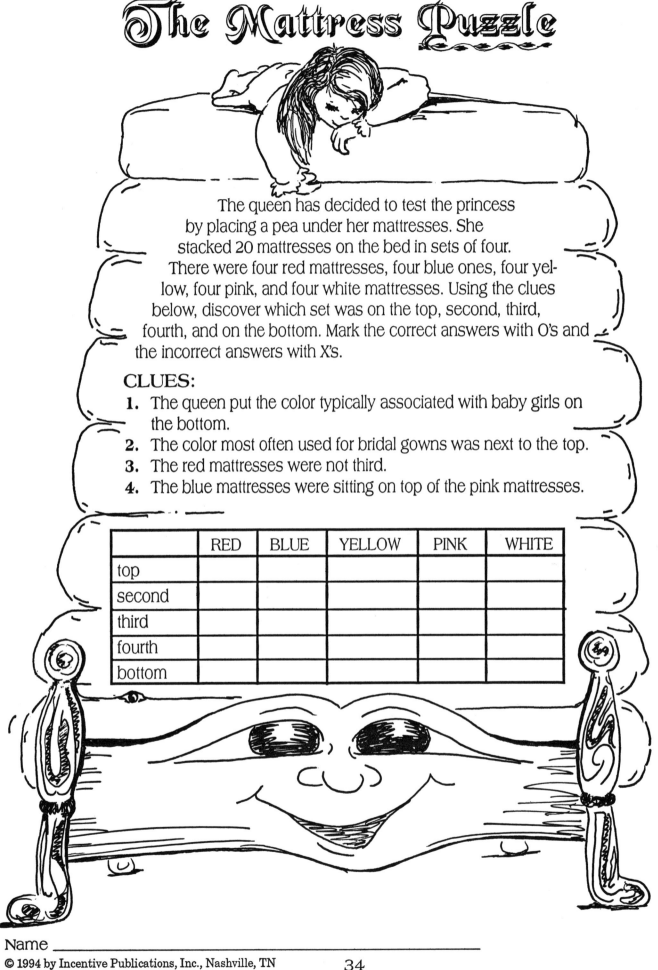

The queen has decided to test the princess by placing a pea under her mattresses. She stacked 20 mattresses on the bed in sets of four. There were four red mattresses, four blue ones, four yellow, four pink, and four white mattresses. Using the clues below, discover which set was on the top, second, third, fourth, and on the bottom. Mark the correct answers with O's and the incorrect answers with X's.

CLUES:

1. The queen put the color typically associated with baby girls on the bottom.
2. The color most often used for bridal gowns was next to the top.
3. The red mattresses were not third.
4. The blue mattresses were sitting on top of the pink mattresses.

	RED	BLUE	YELLOW	PINK	WHITE
top					
second					
third					
fourth					
bottom					

Name _____

Math Puzzles

Here's a pea full of puzzlers for you. How many problems can you solve?

1. $8 \times 2 =$

2. $7 \times 2 =$

3. $2 \times 0 =$

4. $5 \times 2 =$

5. $1 \times 2 =$

6. $4 \times 2 =$

7. $2 \times 6 =$

8. $3 \times 2 =$

9. $11 \times 2 =$

10. $10 \times 2 =$

11. $9 \times 2 =$

12. $2 \times 2 =$

Name _____

Weather Map Symbols for Science Activities

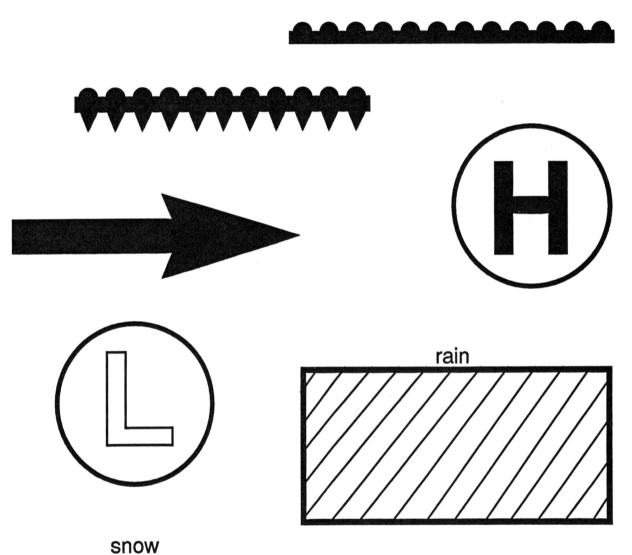

rain

snow

flurries

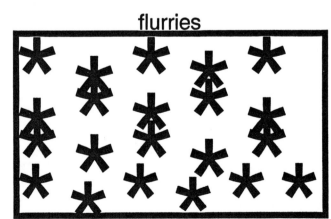

Ticket & Fish Patterns

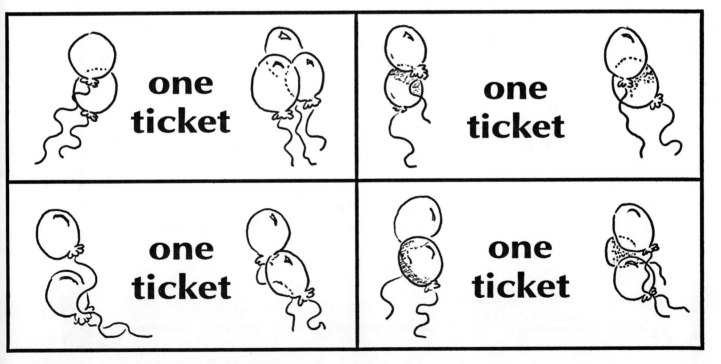

one ticket

one ticket

one ticket

one ticket

The Princess and the Pea

_____

is presented this award
in honor of outstanding and
faithful work on

this _____ day of _____

19 _____

_____

Teacher

Snow White

Snow White

Introductory Activities

1. Introduce the unit by viewing the movie version of *Snow White and the Seven Dwarfs*. Then discuss the movie with the class. **(C) (K)**

2. Pass out copies of *Snow White* for the students to read. Discuss the fairy tale's story-line and look for similarities between the book and the movie. **(C) (K)**

3. Brainstorm to compare and contrast the book and movie versions of *Snow White*. Chart the students' responses. **(C) (AN)**

4. Ask students to evaluate which version they prefer and to write a sentence or two telling why they feel as they do.

Brainstormers

WHAT IF...?

- What if Snow White had not eaten the apple?
- What if Snow White had not fallen in love with the prince upon awakening?
- What if the seven dwarfs had not kept Snow White in their house?

ROLE PLAY
Make stick puppets and act out *Snow White* with the new "What If" endings.
(K) (C) (AP) (FL) (FX) (O) (EL)

Subject Integration

SPELLING & VOCABULARY

SAMPLE VOCABULARY WORDS: *Snow White, apple, kiss, dwarf, queen, mirror, baby, lips, skin, fair, hide, home, bed, woods, mine, comb, blood. Challenge Word: ebony*

Snow White

English

SENTENCE SCRAMBLE

Write a variety of sentences from *Snow White* on 5" x 7" cards, one word per card. To play the game, divide the class into two teams. Give each team five sets of cards. The team first putting the five sentences in order as they appear in the story wins. **(K) (AN)**

CHANGE THAT SENTENCE

Divide the class into five teams. Give each team a copy of *Snow White*. Assign each team to find two sentences which can be changed from statements into questions. To win, the team must be the first to write the two statements and their corresponding questions. **(C) (K)**

Creative Writing

Ask the students to rename the seven dwarfs. As a class project, make a photo-biography gallery of the new seven dwarfs. Trace around the bodies of seven of your students to obtain silhouettes for the dwarfs. While some students are coloring in features and clothes on the dwarfs, others can write the biographies: how the dwarfs got their new names, what types of food they like and dislike, their favorite colors, the sports they like, hobbies, etc. Post the biographies next to the pictures. **(S) (FL) (FX) (O) (EL)**

Game

Select those cards from the Cinderella "Character Match" game (pages 16 and 17) which describe Snow White and her stepmother. **(AP) (AN)**

Snow White

Math

"AND THE WINNER IS . . ."

Discuss the different varieties of apples available at the store. Bring to class a sampling of each kind and let the students taste them. Poll the class to find out which apples they like best and then ask them to make a bar graph showing the poll's results. **(K) (AP) (AN) (E)**

FACTO: A BASIC FACTS GAME

PURPOSE:

To drill basic addition or multiplication facts. The game can be adapted to any skill level and number of players.

PREPARATION:

Cut out the numbered circles provided as patterns (on pages 45 and 46) and laminate them. Place the circles on the classroom wall in a random order.

DIRECTIONS:

Divide the class into two teams. Each player will be blindfolded as he or she takes a turn. Place player within reach of the wall and spin him or her slowly around three times. The player must then attempt to touch a numbered circle. If the player succeeds in contacting at least the edge of a circle, he or she earns one point. If the player can then add (or multiply or subtract) the circle's number to a factor the teacher names, another point will be earned. **(K)**

Health

Discuss the food groups and the components of a balanced meal. Have students plan a day's menu which Snow White could feed to the dwarfs. Let students arrange a bulletin board display picturing their meals. **(K) (C) (AP) (AN) (EL) (FL) (O)**

Snow White

Science

A STUDY OF APPLES

1. Research to discover different varieties of apples. Construct a class book on varieties of apples and apple facts.
2. Research the history of Johnny Appleseed. Role play his life story.
3. Cut up and dry apples. Save dried apple pieces for the Culminating Activity (page 44).

Social Studies

Provide the class with copies of a United States map. Have them label the Great Lakes, the Atlantic and Pacific oceans, the Mississippi River, and the Ohio River. Using a red pen, mark the travels of Johnny Appleseed. (See reproducible map worksheet on page 49). (AP) (AN) (K) (C)

Music

A SALUTE TO SNOW WHITE

Sing these lyrics to the melody of the old English nursery song "The Mulberry Bush."

We're going to keep Snow White safe,
Snow White safe, Snow White safe.
We're going to keep Snow White safe;
The queen will never find her.

What will we do? The queen found her;
The queen found her; the queen found her.
What will we do? The queen found her,
And she ate the poisoned apple!

Let's be happy. Snow White is fine;
Snow White is fine; Snow White is fine.
Let's be happy. Snow White is fine.
The prince was able to cure her!

Snow White

Art

SNOW WHITE'S HOME WITH THE DWARFS

Construct Snow White's home with the dwarfs by using a cardboard stove box obtained from an appliance store. Cut out windows and a door. Let the students design wallpaper for the walls by drawing designs on bulletin board paper. Perhaps some of the older students would like to try to hem some material for curtains. The dwarfs' beds can be made out of shoe boxes and material can be added for bedspreads. A large box can be transformed into a kitchen table. The artists in your room can draw pictures to hang on the walls (framed in tagboard or construction paper, for example). Brick building blocks make a perfect fireplace and chimney.

Planning for Gifted Learners

Suggestions for introducing the gifted learner to logical elimination puzzles are included in the *Cinderella* section (page 15). Two *Snow White* logical elimination puzzles are found on pages 50 and 51. **(AN) (S) (E) (FL)**

Culminating Activity

TASTING PARTY AND WEATHER BOOK

Invite a meteorologist to your classroom (or take a field trip to visit a television station to discuss long-range weather predictions). Have a tasting party while the meteorologist is visiting your class, and serve prepared dried apples, apple pie, apple tarts, apple cookies, caramel apples, and apple cider.

Using the *Farmer's Almanac* as a prototype, put together a class almanac with weather predictions your students write based on the meteorologist's report.

Number Patterns

45

Number Patterns

46

Dwarf Magic

Add these equations:

9 + 2 =_____   2 + 0 =_____   3 + 3 =_____

8 + 3 =_____   4 + 9 =_____   2 + 8 =_____

5 + 4 =_____   6 + 9 =_____   1 + 8 =_____

3 + 5 =_____   8 + 9 =_____   9 + 9 =_____

7 + 6 =_____   5 + 6 =_____   8 + 7 =_____

2 + 7 =_____   7 + 5 =_____   7 + 7 =_____

4 + 8 =_____   9 + 3 =_____   6 + 4 =_____

1 + 9 =_____   9 + 5 =_____   5 + 1 =_____

6 + 8 =_____   7 + 1 =_____   4 + 4 =_____

9 + 7 =_____   8 + 5 =_____   3 + 2 =_____

8 + 0 =_____   5 + 2 =_____   2 + 6 =_____

5 + 5 =_____   6 + 6 =_____   1 + 6 =_____

3 + 4 =_____   3 + 6 =_____

7 + 3 =_____   4 + 7 =_____

Name _____

Apple Equations

1. Johnny went to the store on Tuesday and bought 5 apples that were 10 cents each. How much did Johnny pay for his apples? _____

2. Johnny's sister ate 2 of his apples. How many apples were left for Johnny? _____

3. Johnny's sister bought 4 apples on Wednesday. She paid 20 cents each. How much did she pay for the apples?

4. Who spent more money on apples, Johnny or his sister? How much more? _____

5. Johnny's mother bought a sack of apples to make treats. She made 12 caramel apples and 6 chocolate apples. How many treats did she make in all? _____

6. $6 + 3 =$ ____

7. $2 + 4 + 5 =$ ____

8. $5 +$ ____ $= 8$

9. ____ $+ 4 = 12$

10. ____ $+ 9 = 18$

11. $7 + 8 =$ ____

12. $4 +$ ____ $= 11$

Name _____

Locate your state. Color it yellow.

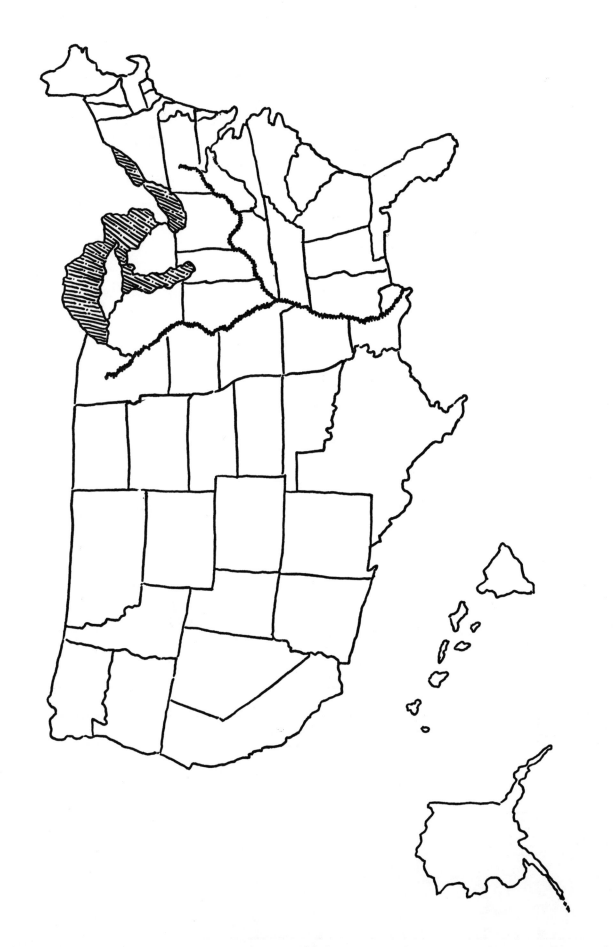

49

Name

The Poisoned Fruit

The wicked queen decided to poison other fruits in case Snow White refused to eat the apple. She put one in a basket, another in a paper bag, another in a box, and one in a velvet bag. Using the clues below find out which fruit she put in each container. Use an O to mark correct answers and an X to mark incorrect answers.

CLUES:
1. The yellow-skinned fruit is in the box.
2. The fuzzy fruit is in the basket.
3. The fruit that grows on a vine is in the paper bag.

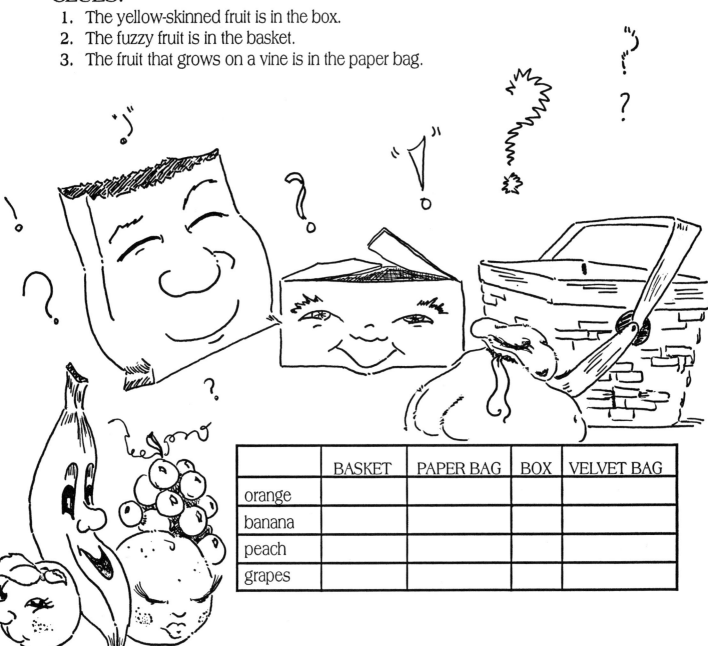

	BASKET	PAPER BAG	BOX	VELVET BAG
orange				
banana				
peach				
grapes				

Name _____

The Mixed-Up Beds

When Snow White was cleaning the dwarfs' house, she moved their beds in order to sweep beneath them. As she was preparing to put the beds back in place, she could remember where only two of the beds went. Dopey's bed was first, and Sleepy's bed was next. Using the clues below, help Snow White find the order to place the other five beds.

CLUES:

1. Grumpy always had to sleep in the middle bed, or he would become grumpy.
2. Doc slept between Grumpy and Bashful.
3. Sneezy slept next to Sleepy.

(Use O's for correct answers and X's for incorrect answers.)

	1	2	3	4	5	6	7
GRUMPY							
SNEEZY							
DOPEY							
BASHFUL							
HAPPY							
DOC							
SLEEPY							

Name _____

You're the ____ of my eye!

Snow White

Apple Sweetone

Excellent Work!

Teacher ____

Sleeping Beauty

Sleeping Beauty

Introductory Activities

1. Turn out the lights and have students place their heads on their desks and nap for ten minutes. "Wake" them by pretending you are a fairy godmother (or godfather!) who taps them on the shoulder with a magic wand. When all of the students are awake, introduce this unit by asking them how it would feel to have slept for 100 years.

2. Brainstorm for ideas on how the world would have changed if everyone in your class had slept for 100 years.

3. Read aloud the story of *Sleeping Beauty* and discuss it with the class.

(AP) (AN) (E) (FL) (FX) (O) (EL)

Brainstormers

WHAT IF...?

- What if the prince had not been able to reach the princess through the thorns?
- What if the prince's kiss had not awakened Sleeping Beauty?

(C) (AP) (S) (FL) (FX) (O) (EL)

Subject Integration

SPELLING & VOCABULARY

SAMPLE VOCABULARY WORDS: *sleeping, castle, prince, mirror, years, awake, hundred, magic, kiss, slept, beauty, princess*

Sleeping Beauty

Drama

Use hand puppets to act out the story incorporating one of the "What If?" changes. **(K) (C) (AP) (FL) (FX) (O) (EL)**

Reading

FALL TREE

Build a colorful autumn scene while learning about root words and affixes. Draw a tree with bare branches and a root system below the ground. Print suffixes and prefixes on colorful leaves. Let the class tape the leaves to the picture—suffixes should be placed on the ground around the tree and prefixes should be placed on the tree's limbs. Have cards prepared with root words on them to tape across the roots of your tree. Make a game of taking the cards and leaves off the tree and matching the root words to the proper affixes. **(K) (C)**

MAIN IDEA

Select several paragraphs from *Sleeping Beauty* and write them on index cards. Laminate the cards for durability. As each student selects a card, have him or her write the main idea of each paragraph. **(K) (C)**

English

REMEMBER THAT VERB

Adapt the game of Simon Says to a game using verb recognition as the key to determine whether to stand or sit.

VERB SEARCH

Pass out the index cards from the previous reading activity and have students locate the verbs. Then assign them to write original sentences with the verbs they found. **(C) (AP) (O) (EL) (FL)**

Sleeping Beauty

 ath

"PAIR" TREE

PURPOSE:
To teach the associative property of multiplication and to drill multiplication facts

OBJECT:
To gain the most points by making correct matches of pairs of facts (game can be adapted for drill of addition facts)

MATERIALS:
- posterboard for pear tree shape (see pattern on page 61)
- 20–25 pairs of pear-shaped cards for math equations (see pattern on page 62)

DIRECTIONS:
Shuffle game cards. Lay cards on table facing up and in random order. The first player picks a card and says the product (or sum). If the player's answer is correct, he or she may lay the card on a pear in the tree and receive one point. If he or she can find the other card which has the same product (or sum) and lay it on the matching pear, he or she will earn two points. Play proceeds to the right until all game cards have been used. If a player gives an incorrect answer, he or she must put the card back on the table.

Sample Equations:

2 x 2	4 x 1 OR	4 + 2	5 + 1
3 x 2	6 x 1	3 + 4	5 + 2
4 x 2	8 x 1	8 + 4	6 + 6
3 x 3	9 x 1	6 + 8	10 + 4
6 x 2	4 x 3	7 + 9	8 + 8

Try mixing some problems for challenging those gifted in math.

Example:

4 x 2	5 + 3
3 x 1	9 ÷ 3
3 x 2	12 − 6
4 + 5	15 − 6

Sleeping Beauty

Social Studies

EUROPEAN CASTLE LIFE DURING THE MIDDLE AGES

Assign students to research groups. Each group will attempt to research one of the following topics:

- How were European medieval castles designed and built?
- What kind of food was served in the medieval castle?
- How did Europeans dress during the Middle Ages?

Group 1 will build a castle. Group 2 will draw a mural to show a banquet scene in the great hall. Group 3 will make paper dolls and dress them in medieval dress.

Art

In connection with the Social Studies focus on castle life, have students build a castle. This may be a group or individual project.

Music

Use the melody of the old French round "Are You Sleeping, Brother John?" to sing this song.

Are You Sleeping, Princess Dear?

Are you sleeping, are you sleeping,
Princess dear, princess dear?
"Let me kiss your cheek now.
Let me kiss your cheek now,"
Said the prince, said the prince.

After the class learns the new words to the song, let them sing it as a round.

Creative Writing

Assign students to write a paragraph explaining how to cast a spell like the one the wicked fairy cast on Sleeping Beauty. They should then write another paragraph telling how a good fairy could undo the bad spell. (K) (C) (S) (FL) (FX) (O) (EL)

Sleeping Beauty

Science

LEAF ALBUM

As a class project, collect different varieties of leaves. Press, mount, and label leaves to make a leaf album.

DECIDUOUS AND EVERGREEN TREES

Let each student select a favorite tree to research, collecting data about its leaves, seeds, bark, height, habitat, etc. Help each design a project which will best present his or her information: a report, diorama, booklet, poster, flip book, etc. **(K) (C) (AP) (S) (EL) (O) (FL) (FX)**

ACTIVITY EXTENSION

Have students draw several one-inch-size pictures of their trees. On a world map, have them place their trees wherever that kind of tree grows. **(K) (C) (AP)**

Planning for Gifted Learning

1. Assign students to draw mazes to accompany the fairy tale. Make copies of their mazes and distribute to the class for students to work.
2. Students complete the logical elimination puzzle (see page 63).

(AP) (AN) (E) (FL) (FX) (O) (EL)

Culminating Activity

SCAVENGER HUNT: *An Activity Based on Cinderella, Snow White, and Sleeping Beauty*

Divide the class into scavenger groups, each with a list of items to locate. Establish rules to govern the search and list the categories for which you will give prizes. Suggested search time: 30 minutes. Items numbered 1–6 require objects to be located. Items numbered 7–31 require word cards. Write words on 5" x 7" index cards or tagboard circles. Clues are listed on page 59. Scavenger hunt materials and words are listed on page 60.

Sleeping Beauty

CLUES

1. Find one object which is the same color as Snow White's hair.
2. Find one object which is the same color as Snow White's lips.
3. Find one object which is made from the same material as Cinderella's slippers.
4. Find the first thing the wicked queen poisoned when she tried to hurt Snow White.
5. Find the object which told Snow White's stepmother she was not the fairest of them all.
6. Find the poisoned fruit which Snow White ate.
7. Find a word card which names the food that Cinderella's horses ate before they became horses.
8. Find a word card which names the food that Cinderella's footman ate before he was changed into a footman.
9. Was Snow White's stepmother a queen? Find a word card which answers this question.
10. Find as many cards as you can which name the seven dwarfs.
11. Find a word card which names the fruit used for Cinderella's coach.
12. Find a word card which names the material used to make the dwarfs' beds.
13. Find a word card which names the number of dwarfs in *Snow White*.
14. Find a word card which lists the curse the wicked fairy gave Sleeping Beauty.
15. Find a word card which tells how many stepsisters Cinderella has.
16. Find a word card which tells what grew up around the castle where Sleeping Beauty slept.
17. Find a word card which tells how many years Sleeping Beauty slept.
18. Find a word card that names the person who awakened Sleeping Beauty.
19. Find a word card which tells what the prince did to save Snow White's life.
20. Find a word card which tells the time Cinderella had to leave the ball.
21. Find a word card which names a fairy tale character who had a stepmother. (Two possible answers.)
22. Find a word card which tells the age Sleeping Beauty would be when the curse would fall upon her.
23. Find a card which names the person whom the queen told to kill Snow White.
24. Find a word card which tells what Sleeping Beauty's father tried to destroy so that she would never see one during her lifetime.
25. Find a word which tells how Sleeping Beauty was awakened.
26. Find a word card which tells where the dwarfs in Snow White worked.
27. Find a word card which tells the kind of home in which Sleeping Beauty lived.
28. Find a word card which tells how many brothers and sisters Cinderella has.
29. Find a word card which names the material which was used to make Snow White's coffin.
30. Was Cinderella's stepmother a queen? Find a word card which answers this question.

Sleeping Beauty

MATERIALS AND WORD CARDS NEEDED FOR SCAVENGER HUNT

Materials:
1. black object
2. comb
3. red object
4. mirror
5. small baby food jar
6. apple

Word Card Word List:
7. oats
8. cheese
9. yes
10. Grumpy, Sneezy, Doc, Dopey, Bashful, Happy, Sleepy
11. pumpkin
12. wood
13. seven
14. She will prick her finger on a spindle and die.
15. two
16. thorn forest
17. 100 years
18. prince
19. move Snow White's coffin
20. twelve o'clock
21. Snow White/Cinderella
22. 16 years
23. huntsman
24. all spinning wheels and spindles
25. a kiss
26. a mine
27. a castle
28. none
29. glass
30. no

— Where's the cheese?

Pair Tree

Pair Patterns

Larger patterns are for use with class game.

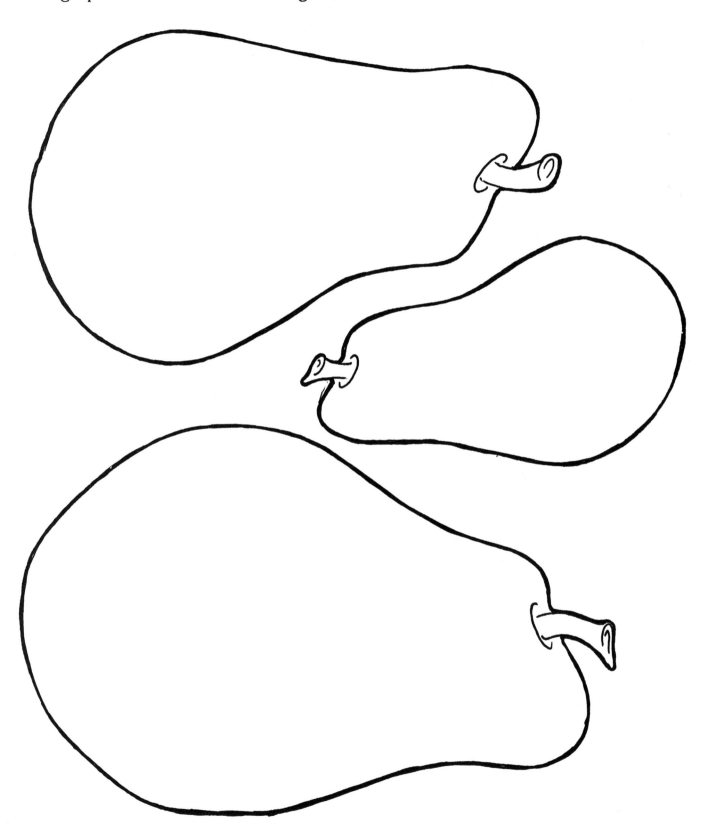

The Royal Parties

Sleeping Beauty has been invited to four parties. The parties are being hosted by a duke, an earl, a king, and a prince. Sleeping Beauty's only problem is deciding on which gown to wear to each party. Her choices are a blue velvet, a green velvet, a red taffeta, and a purple silk. Using the clues below, match the parties with the gowns. Use O's for correct answers and X's for incorrect answers.

CLUES

1. The prince's favorite color is the color of the sky.
2. The earl's hair is the same color as this gown.
3. Sleeping Beauty will wear a "royal" color to the king's ball.

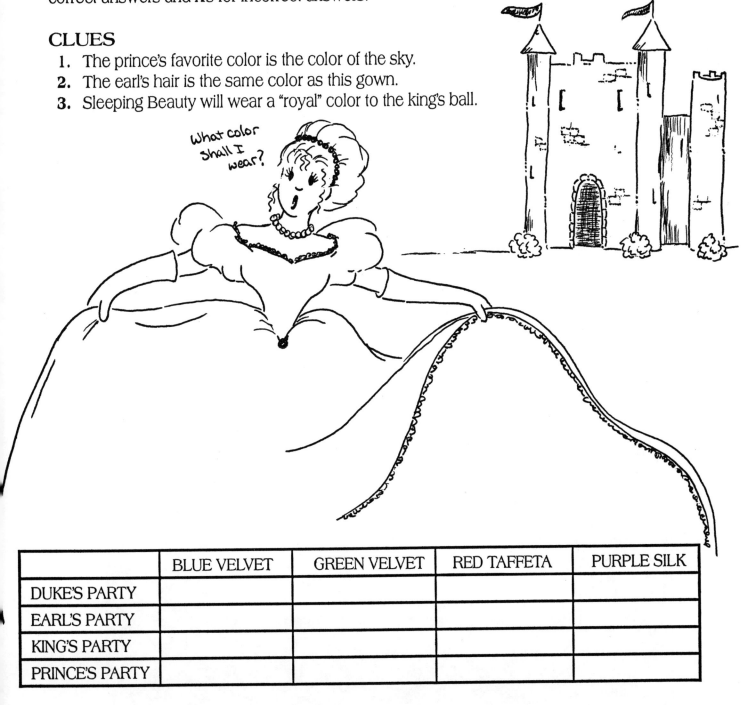

What color shall I wear?

	BLUE VELVET	GREEN VELVET	RED TAFFETA	PURPLE SILK
DUKE'S PARTY				
EARL'S PARTY				
KING'S PARTY				
PRINCE'S PARTY				

Name _____

Sleeping Beauty

Congratulations

_____

on

your

good work!

_____
Teacher

The Little Mermaid

The Little Mermaid

Introductory Activities

1. Show the movie version of *The Little Mermaid* and discuss it with the class.
2. Read the book version of the story. Compare and contrast the versions.
3. Evaluate the class's favorite version.

(K) (C) (E)

Brainstormers

WHAT IF...?

- What if the Little Mermaid had been able to talk when she arrived on land?
- What if the Little Mermaid had never reached land?

ROLE PLAY

Ask for volunteers to role play one of the "What If?" ideas.

Subject Integration

SPELLING & VOCABULARY

SAMPLE VOCABULARY WORDS: *sea, mermaid, treasure, talk, land, little, shell, ocean, wave, kingdom, fish, water, starfish, crab*

Creative Writing

MERMAID KINGDOM NEWSPAPER

As a class writing project, put together a newspaper in which every feature, ad, editorial, comic, etc, is based on *The Little Mermaid* or on some aspect of the ocean kingdom.

The Little Mermaid

Reading

"VOWEL A" MOBILES

Let students make mobiles, using sea animals or shells as their basic design elements. On the front of each piece, write a word with a vowel A sound. On the back of each piece, write the phonetic symbol for that sound above the letter A. **(K) (AN)**

VOWELS TREASURE CHEST

Decorate a box to resemble a treasure chest. Place in it familiar objects. Let the students pull out a treasure, name it, and then name the vowel sound in the initial syllable of the word. **(K) (AN)**

English

SEA TREASURE: AN ADJECTIVE GAME

Divide the class into three to four teams. Give each team a treasure sack containing word cards that name items related to the sea. Assign the teams to examine their cards and to brainstorm for as many adjectives as they can produce which describe each card. After each team shares its list, award prizes to the team which listed the most adjectives per card. **(K)**

FAIRY TALE PASSWORD

Divide the class into two teams. Using vocabulary words from the fairy tales, play a game of Fairy Tale Password. To play, students guess vocabulary words from clues which you supply. Award ten points for an answer reached on the first clue, nine points for an answer reached on the second clue, and eight points for an answer reached on the third and final clue.

The Little Mermaid

Math

SHELL EQUATIONS

Using sea shells, let students solve addition (or any other math operation you choose) equations by arranging shells in the pattern needed to solve the problems. If real shells are unavailable, cut shell patterns out of construction paper and laminate. **(K) (AP)**

For additional math practice, refer to reproducible math activity on page 71.

Science

OCEANOGRAPHY

Place students in cooperative research groups.

GROUP ONE: What kinds of mammals live in the ocean? List as many as you can find. Choose three to research in detail.

GROUP TWO: What kind of fish live in the ocean? List as many as you can find. Choose three to research in detail.

GROUP THREE: Research the octopus and the squid. Compare and contrast the two animals.

Assign the groups to produce an oral report using visual displays of their choice.

FOSSIL SEA SHELLS

Mix plaster of paris. Fill small plastic cups which have been greased with petroleum jelly to their halfway mark with the plaster mixture. Coat the bottom of a shell with petroleum jelly. Press the shell into the plaster to make a fossil imprint. Remove shell when plaster is almost hard. After the plaster has hardened, tear away the paper cup and view the fossil imprint.

(K) (C) (AP) (S) (O) (EL) (FL)

The Little Mermaid

Social Studies

Play a game of Tic Tac Toe to teach students to locate and name the oceans of the world, the Gulf of Mexico, and the Great Lakes of the United States of America. Use the acronym HOMES (Huron, Ontario, Michigan, Erie, Superior) to aid in the name recall of the Great Lakes.

To play, follow the traditional rules of Tic Tac Toe, with the exception that in order to place an X or an O on the game board, the team (or player) must correctly answer a question. **(K)**

Sample Questions:
- Name the Great Lake which begins with the letter H.
- Name the Great Lake which begins with the letter O.
- Name the Great Lake which begins with the letter M.
- Name the Great Lake which begins with the letter E.
- Name the Great Lake which begins with the letter S.
- Name the ocean which touches California.
- Name the ocean which touches Virginia.
- Name the ocean which is on the eastern side of the United States of America.
- Name the ocean which is on the western side of the United States of America.
- Name the ocean which is at the North Pole.
- Name the ocean which is near Antarctica.
- Name the ocean which is on the eastern side of Africa.
- Name the gulf which lies below the United States of America.

Art

While studying the ocean, tempera paints can be used to create wonderful ocean scene paintings. Frame students' work with construction paper frames for display. Scatter some cutouts of fish, starfish, etc., throughout the display to create a seaside atmosphere.

The Little Mermaid

Music

Sing these new words to the old nursery song "Ten Little Indians."

Ten Wiggly Fishes

One wiggly, two wiggly, three wiggly fishes,
Four wiggly, five wiggly, six wiggly fishes,
Seven wiggly, eight wiggly, nine wiggly fishes,
Ten wiggly fishes swimming in a row.

As students sing, have them hold their hands in
front of their bodies and push outward horizontally
as if gliding through the water.

Planning for Gifted Learners

Two logical elimination puzzles are provided with this unit. (See pages 72 and 73.)

Culminating Activity

3-D MURAL

Divide the class into four work groups. Provide each with long strips of bulletin board
paper. Assign the groups to paint an ocean background using tempera paints. Place
ocean plant and animal life made from construction paper on the mural to make a 3-D
scene. After murals are hung, groups can hang paper fish on string from the ceiling so
that they float in front of the mural, giving it an added three-dimensional effect.

Fishing for Answers

1. The Little Mermaid found 3 pink shells on Monday, 9 white shells on Tuesday, and 4 yellow shells on Wednesday. How many shells did she find in all? _____

2. How many more shells did she find on Tuesday than on Monday?_____

3. 13 small fish were swimming near a coral reef. A large grouper came along and ate 8 of the fish. How many fish were left? _____

4. Pirate Jack was fishing for his dinner. He caught 8 fish yesterday. Today he caught twice as many fish as he did yesterday. How many fish did he catch today?_____

5. There were 10 dolphins swimming together in the Atlantic Ocean. Later 8 more dolphins joined the group. After swimming together for one hour, 4 dolphins left the group. How many dolphins were left? _____

Name _____

Ahoy, Mates!

The Little Mermaid is quite upset. She has lost four items: a pearl necklace, a gold ring, a silver comb, and an ivory brush. She has looked for them everywhere. Help her find the items by using the clues below to match them with the places they are located: a sunken ship, an oyster shell, a treasure chest, and in the sea coral. Use O's to mark correct answers.

CLUES:

1. The oyster cannot claim the pearls.
2. The silver comb is in a box.
3. An animal has the pearl necklace.
4. The ivory brush lies near the mast.

	SUNKEN SHIP	OYSTER SHELL	TREASURE CHEST	SEA CORAL
pearl necklace				
gold ring				
silver comb				
ivory brush				

Name _____

The Diver's Dilemma

A diver was swimming in the ocean to photograph marine life for a magazine. He was looking for a school of fish, an electric eel, a manta ray, a shark, and an octopus. They were located under a rock, beside a coral reef, near the surface of the water, in a sunken ship, and hiding in the sand. Help the diver take his photographs by locating each animal or group of animals. Mark correct answers with O's and incorrect answers with X's.

CLUES:
1. The octopus was swimming in what was once the captain's quarters.
2. The fish were not hiding in the sand or under a rock.
3. The shark could see sunlight.
4. The electric eel hates sand because it gets in his eyes.

	UNDER A ROCK	BESIDE A CORAL REEF	IN A SUNKEN SHIP	HIDING IN SAND	ON THE SURFACE OF WATER
FISH					
ELECTRIC EEL					
MANTA RAY					
SHARK					
OCTOPUS					

Name _____

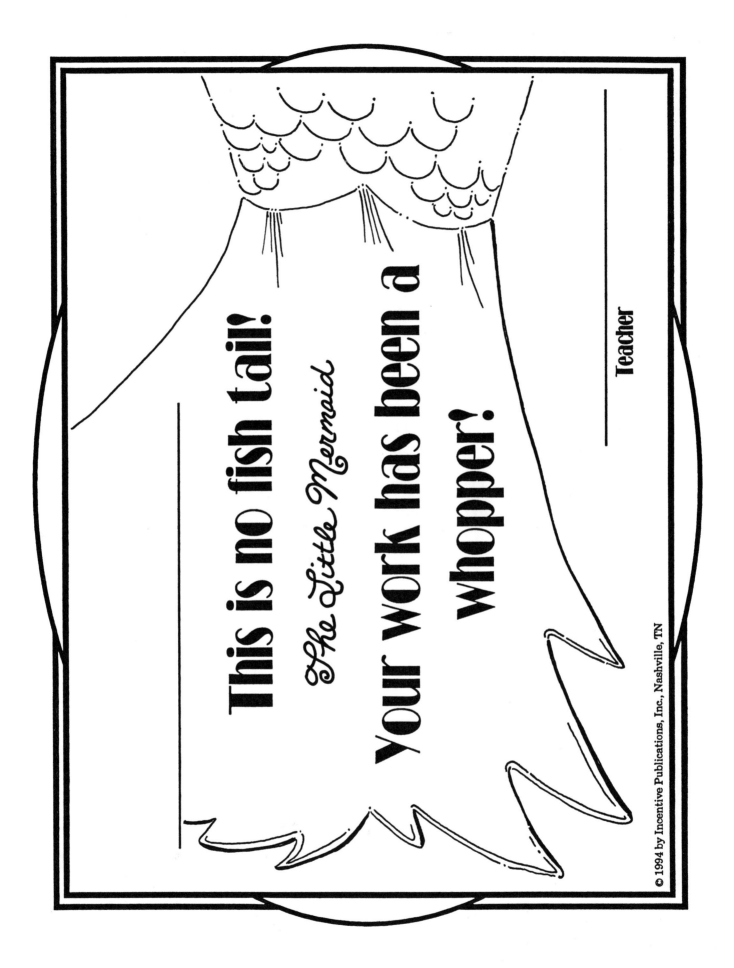

This is no fish tail!

The Little Mermaid

Your work has been a whopper!

Teacher

Rapunzel

Rapunzel

Introductory Activities

1. Bring to class enough rope to make a fifteen-foot braid. The rope should be partially braided. Invite a guest to visit your class to read aloud *Rapunzel* while you continue to braid the rope. Allow some of the students to finish the braid. Hang the braid on the wall to illustrate how the witch and the prince climbed into the tower.

2. Discuss the story of *Rapunzel* with the class. Ask the students to select and share their favorite parts of the story. Ask why Rapunzel's mother had such a craving for the rapunzel lettuce. **(K) (C)**

Brainstormers

WHAT IF...?

- What if Rapunzel's hair had not grown long? How could the witch have climbed into the tower?
- What if Rapunzel had not given away the fact that she had a secret visitor?
- What if Rapunzel's mother had never wanted to eat the rapunzel lettuce?

(C) (AP) (S) (FL) (O) (EL)

Subject Integration

SPELLING & VOCABULARY

SAMPLE VOCABULARY WORDS: *rope, hair, braid, wall, prince, tower, lettuce, long, grown, grow, climb, mother, witch, forest, escape, comb*

Rapunzel

 **eading**

STUDY AREA: BLENDS

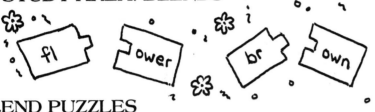

BLEND PUZZLES

Cut out rectangle shapes on large index cards or pieces of tagboard. Cut each rectangle into two interlocking puzzle pieces. Print a blend on one half of the puzzle piece and the rest of the word on the other. Laminate the puzzle pieces and place them in a box. Make a game of finding the matching pieces. *See page 81 for puzzle piece patterns.* **(K)**

STAND-UP BLENDS

Instruct the students to listen as you call out a list of words. Each time the students hear a word with a blend, they will stand up. **(K)**

BEAN BAG TOSS

Materials Needed: • posterboard • bean bag • box
• word cards with vocabulary words containing blends

Draw a large bull's-eye target on a piece of posterboard, labeling each section with numbers. These numbers will correspond with the amount of points allotted to each section. Put it on the floor and use masking tape to mark off a place on which students should stand. The object of the game is to toss the bean bag at the center of the target. In order to obtain the points they hit with their bean bags, students must draw a word card from a box, pronounce the word, and name its blend. **(K)**

 nglish

SUBJECT & PREDICATE MATCH GAME

Make two interlocking puzzle parts out of tagboard. Print a subject on one puzzle piece and a predicate on the other. Use sentences from *Rapunzel*. Students try to match the subject and predicate pairs. *See page 82 for puzzle piece patterns.* **(K) (C)**

Rapunzel

Creative Writing

Pretend that a wicked witch locked you in a tower deep within a forest so that no one could find you. Write a story about how you managed to escape. Draw a map of the forest and show your escape route. Include on the map the dangerous areas through which you had to walk. **(AP) (AN) (S) (FL) (FX) (O) (EL)**

Math

STUDY: MEASUREMENT

1. Measure the length of the rope braid which you made.

2. Rapunzel's tower is thirteen feet tall. Measure this length on the classroom floor.

3. Rapunzel's tower is six feet wide. Measure this width on the classroom floor.

MEASUREMENT HUNT

Select several items in your room which the students could measure, such as a book, the teacher's desk, a table, a bookcase, a rug or carpet square, the chalk tray, a pencil, etc. Students list their measurements on a sheet of paper. **(K) (C) (AP)**

Rapunzel

Science

STUDY: HAIR AND HAIR CARE

1. Research to discover facts about human hair.
2. Discuss different methods of hair care, such as brushing and washing.
3. Look at hair under a microscope.
4. Measure the average length of a strand of hair.

"HAIRY" FAMILY TREE POSTERS

Ask parents to help their students research their own family trees, including a listing of the hair colors of their parents, grandparents, and any other close relatives they know. Assist students in designing their family trees. Some may wish to include photos or drawings of their relatives to show their exact hair colors. (K) (AP)

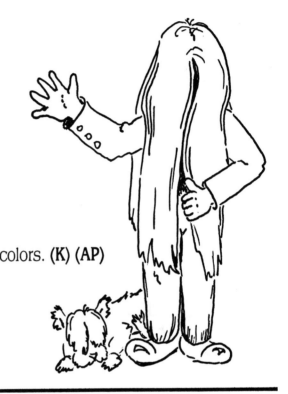

Social Studies

STUDY: JAKOB AND WILHELM GRIMM'S GERMANY

Assign students to research groups. Each group should produce a poster depicting the facts which they have discovered. (K) (C) (AP) (EL) (FL)

Group One: Who are Jakob and Wilhelm Grimm?

Group Two: What is the Black Forest? Where is it located? Why is it famous?

Group Three: Locate the following facts about Germany: its capital, language, chief farm products, money, and the colors and design of its flag.

Rapunzel

Games

LEARNING CENTER

Make up question cards based on the fairy tales you have studied to use with games such as Candyland and other popular board games. Before a player can move on the board, he or she must correctly answer a question. **(K)**

Art

Assign students to draw a picture based on some aspect of *Rapunzel*. Collect the drawings and compile them into a book to share with another class.

Planning for Gifted Learners

1. A reproducible logical elimination puzzle is included with the unit (page 83).
2. Assign students to design a puzzle of their own choosing. Place puzzles in the learning center.

(AP) (AN) (S) (FL) (FX) (O) (EL) (E)

Culminating Activity

GAME PARTY

In pairs, students create original games based on *Rapunzel* or on information from the social studies research activity. Host a game party and let students play the games. Ask parent volunteers to help you make and serve traditional German treats.

Blend Puzzles

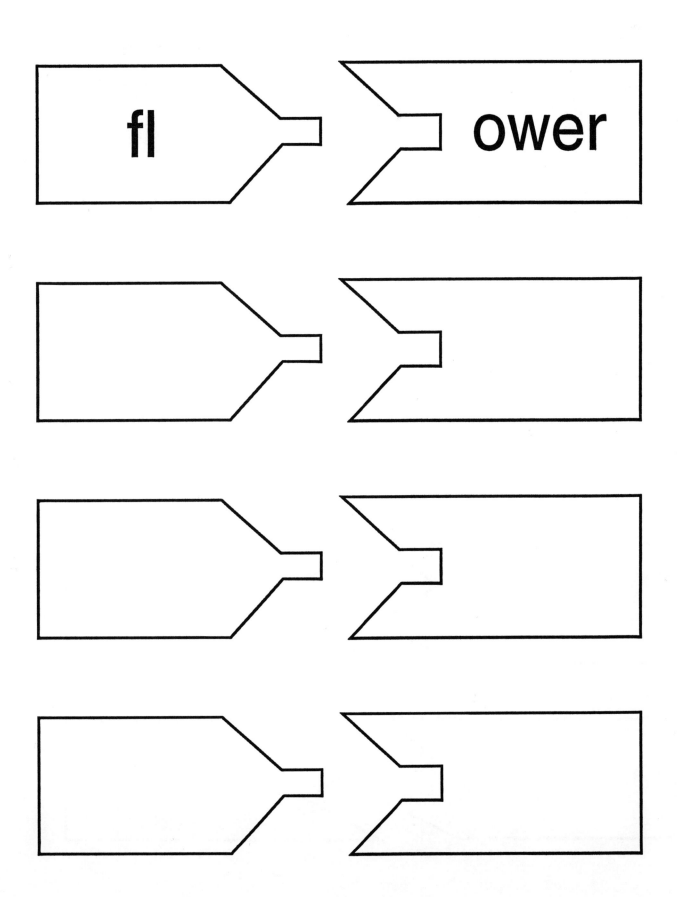

fl

ower

Subject & Predicate Match

Then she | let down her braid.

The Friends' Favorite Flowers

Rapunzel worked every day in her flower garden before she was locked in the tower. She loved to give the flowers to her friends, Mary, Joan, Marta, and Carol. Rapunzel grew roses, tulips, carnations, and petunias. Using the clues below, match the flowers to her friends. Write an O for each correct answer and an X for each incorrect answer.

CLUES

1. The name of Carol's flowers begin with the same letter as her name.

2. Mary's flowers bloom only in the spring.

3. Marta likes the poem "_____ are red. Violets are blue . . ." because it reminds her of her favorite flowers.

	MARY	JOAN	MARTA	CAROL
roses				
tulips				
carnations				
petunias				

Name _____

Rapunzel says, "Super Work !"

Teacher

Beauty and the Beast

Beauty and the Beast

Introductory Activities

1. Find someone who can dress up in a gorilla costume to visit your classroom. While the beast is present, read aloud the story of *Beauty and the Beast*.

2. If you have more than one version of *Beauty and the Beast*, read all versions and ask the class to compare and contrast the versions using brainstorming techniques.

3. View the movie version of *Beauty and the Beast* and compare it with the book version.

4. Ask students to evaluate their favorite version, telling what they liked best and least about it and why. **(K) (C) (E)**

Brainstormers

WHAT IF...?

- What if Beauty was so afraid of the beast that she refused to return to his home?

- What if Beauty had refused to live with the beast at all?

- What if the spell had not been broken? What else could have been done to break it?
(C) (AP) (S) (EL) (O) (FL) (FX)

Reading

STUDY: BEGINNING SOUNDS OF WORDS

HANGMAN

Place the class into teams. Play a game of Hangman by giving each team a word and asking them to identify its beginning consonant sound(s). Each team must correctly identify the beginning sounds of six words to keep the hangman from being drawn. A team's turn lasts until the complete hangman is drawn. Teams can receive one point per word correctly identified.
(C) (K) (AN)

Subject Integration

SPELLING & VOCABULARY

SAMPLE VOCABULARY WORDS: *beauty, beast, afraid, home, refuse, spell, change, become, see, character, beastly, face, animal*

Beauty and the Beast

English

STUDY: CORRECT VERB USAGE

TOWER BLOCKS GAME MATCH

Draw a large tower on a piece of posterboard. Cut out blocks from red construction paper. (Cut enough blocks to cover your tower.) Print verb pairs on each block, such as *have seen, saw; has gone, went;* etc. Make up a series of sentences using one of the verbs in each verb pair. As students read a sentence, they decide which verb is the correct response by placing their choice on the tower. **(K) (C)**

EASTER EGG MATCH GAME

Write sentences on small strips of paper, leaving out the verb. Place each strip of paper in a plastic egg stored in a basket. Make four to five large signs on which you print a verb you are teaching. To play the game, the student will open the egg, read the sentence, and place the strip upon the sign which displays the verb that correctly completes that sentence. If played competitively, points can be taken for the student who correctly identifies the most verbs. **(K) (C)**

Creative Writing

DIARY ENTRIES

CHOOSE ONE:

1. Pretend you are the beast and explain in your diary how you felt when you were changed into a beast. Describe the problems you had after you became a beast.

2. Pretend you are Beauty. Write in your diary about how you felt when you had to go live with the beast. Describe what it was like to live in his house.

(O) (EL) (FL) (FX)

Beauty and the Beast

Creative Writing

USING COUPLETS

Poets often use couplets when writing a long poem. Read aloud examples of poems that use couplets, discussing the poems' rhyme patterns. Some suggestions include "Holding Hands" by Lenore M. Link, "The Elf and the Doormouse" by Oliver Herford, "If I Were a King" by A. A. Milne, and "A Calendar" by Sara Coleridge. **(S) (O) (FL) (EL) (FX)**

Brainstorm to complete these lines.

1. I saw a plane up in the sky
   _____

   Where it is going I do not know
   _____
   _____

2. If I could be a witch who flies
   _____

   I'd scare my friends on Halloween night
   _____

3. My eyes are blue as blue can be,
   My nose is bigger than a tree.
   _____
   _____

Assign students to write a two-stanza poem using couplets. Starter suggestions:
- My cat is as funny as he (she) can be...
- My dog is as smart as she (he) can be...
- I love to eat...
- I'd like to...
- I often wish I were a...

Math

ON YOUR TOES (A MULTIPLICATION GAME)

Your class will have to be "on their toes" to play this basic facts drill game. Seat the players in a circle. The object of the game is to be able to give the product of a multiplication problem when the bean bag is tossed to you. To begin the play, state which multiplication table will be used (for example, the 3s). Call out a factor (for example, 5) and then toss the bean bag to a child. Whoever catches the bag gives the product of the number you called and the number of the multiplication table you chose (for example, 3 x 5 equals 15). The game continues as the player who caught the bag calls out another number and tosses the bag to another student. When the 3 multiplication table has been exhausted, announce the new table to be used and continue the game.

3 x 5 = 15!

EXTENSION:

Use the game to drill addition facts by stating that all numbers will be added to a number you designate.

See math worksheet on page 92.

Game

FAIRY TALE TIC TAC TOE

Write a list of questions based on the fairy tales you have studied. In order to be able to mark an X or an O on the board, students must correctly answer one of the questions. **(K)**

Beauty and the Beast

Science

STUDY: BUFFALOES

Introduce the study of mammals, concentrating on buffaloes. Assign two-member teams to research facts about the buffalo. Have the teams present their facts in a visual form, such as an illustrated report, a poster, diorama, etc. **(K) (C) (AP) (AN) (S) (FL) (FX) (O) (EL)**

Art

STUDY: BUILDING A MODEL OF A PLAINS INDIAN VILLAGE

Materials Needed:
- markers
- string
- popsicle sticks
- glue
- crayons or tempera paint
- brown paper bags (one bag per four students)

Cut apart large brown paper bags into four equally-sized sheets. Each student takes a sheet and crushes it into a ball. The students will continue to pull their balls apart and crush them until the paper becomes soft and pliable like cloth. Instruct each student to smooth out his or her sheet and paint Native American designs on it. Students will then construct tepees from their papers. Assemble the Native American village on a large piece of green bulletin board paper. Add the tepees and other details such as a stream, trees, animals, cooking fires, etc., to give the scene a realistic look.

Social Studies

STUDY: HOW THE NATIVE AMERICANS USED THE BUFFALO

Let the students research to find out how important the buffalo was to the Plains Indians. Add to your Native American village a rack for drying buffalo skins and any other ways the students can think of that shows how the Indians made use of the buffalo.

Invite other classes to view your village. Have the students prepare oral reports and illustrated posters showing what they have learned about the buffalo. **(K) (C) (AP) (AN) (O) (FL) (EL)**

Beauty and the Beast

Planning for Gifted Learners

1. Reproduce the logical elimination puzzle on page 93 for gifted learners.

2. Assign gifted students to construct a crossword puzzle (or other puzzle) using questions based on the fairy tales you have covered. Put puzzles in a learning center for the class to work during free time.

(C) (AP) (EL) (O) (FL) (FX) (AN) (S) (E)

Culminating Activities

BEAUTY AND THE BEAST CUBES

Students make giant cubes from pieces of posterboard taped together. Each side of the cube will depict a scene from *Beauty and the Beast* or from your Native American/buffalo study.

BLAST OFF VIDEO TAPING PARTY

End your study of fairy tales with a blast! Throw a Fairy Tale Characters Party at which students dress as their favorite fairy tale characters. Videotape each student as he or she tells something about him- or herself. Invite parents and display the Native American village and *Beauty and the Beast* cubes.

Beastly Problems

1. Beauty decided to have fresh flowers on the dinner table. She went to the garden and cut 8 red roses, 6 pink carnations, and 12 daisies. How many flowers did she cut in all? _____

   A dozen flowers fell in the fish pond before she reached the house. How many flowers did she have left? _____

   It takes 30 flowers to fill the large vase. How many more flowers will she need to fill the large vase? _____

Figure out each number pattern and fill in the blanks.

2. 2 4 6 8 __ __ __ __

3. 4 8 __ 16 13 10 __ __

4. 10 __ 30 40 35 __ 25 __

Complete the magic circles by making each horizontal, vertical, and diagonal row add up to the same sum.

5.

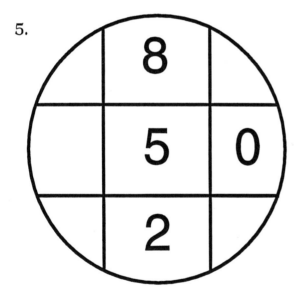

6.

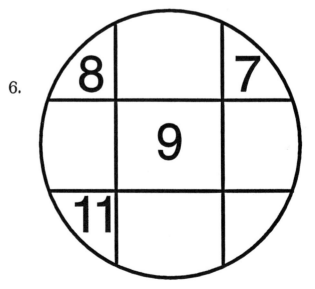

The Beast Dines Tonight

The Beast asked Beauty to invite company for dinner on Monday, Tuesday, Saturday, and Sunday. He wanted to serve lamb chops, steak, ham, and chicken. Using the clues below, discover the dish served on each day. Mark each correct answer with an O and each incorrect answer with an X.

CLUES

1. On the first day of the weekend, Beauty served ham.
2. Chicken was served on a school day.
3. Steak was served on the day after chicken was served.

	LAMB CHOPS	STEAK	HAM	CHICKEN
Monday				
Tuesday				
Saturday				
Sunday				

Name _____

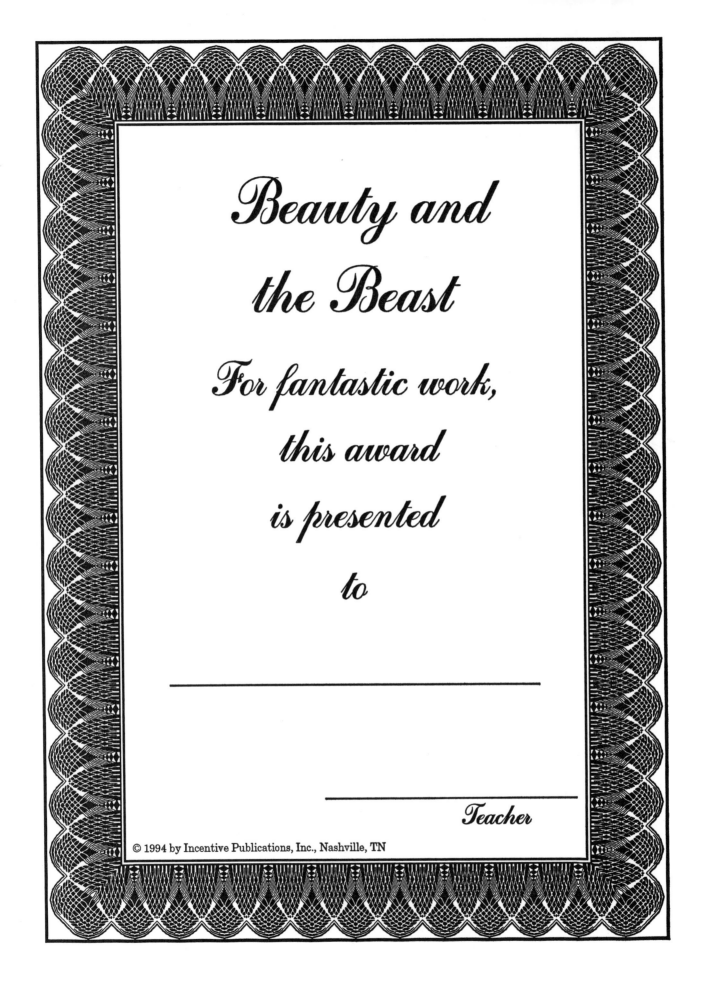

Beauty and the Beast

For fantastic work, this award is presented to

_____

_____

Teacher

PAGE 13–CHARACTER MATCH GAME
Stepmother: old, cruel, greedy, ugly, favored her own daughters
Fairy Godmother: kind, helpful, knows magic, generous
Cinderella: sweet, loving, young, pretty, hard-working, uncomplaining, cheerful
Stepsisters: lazy, mean, jealous, spoiled
Prince: king's son, honorable, handsome, in love with Cinderella, looking for a wife, rich

PAGE 18–PUMPKIN QUEST
1. 12 **2.** 10 **3.** 6 **4.** 8 **5.** 10 **6.** 6
7. 8 **8.** 9 **9.** 8 **10.** 6 **11.** 9 **12.** 8

PAGE 19–CHORE TIME
mop, barn; bucket, bedroom; broom, back-yard; dust rags, garden

PAGE 20–MEET THE PRINCE
first, Janet; second, Mary; third, Anna; last, Elizabeth

PAGE 21–THE BALL GOWN MYSTERY
Mary, blue; Janet, pink; Elizabeth, green; Anna, red

PAGE 33–A PRICKLY PRINCESS PUZZLE
1. bed, bee, fee, fed
    rain, rail, tail, toil, boil
    pea, tea, tee, bee, fee
    blue, glue, glee, flee
2. bold, cold, fold, gold, hold, mold, sold, told
3. bump, dump, hump, jump, lump, pump, tump

PAGE 34–THE MATTRESS PUZZLE
top, red; second, white; third, yellow; fourth, blue; bottom, pink

PAGE 35–MATH PUZZLES
1. 16 **2.** 14 **3.** 0 **4.** 10 **5.** 2 **6.** 8
7. 12 **8.** 6 **9.** 22 **10.** 20 **11.** 18
12. 4

PAGE 47 – DWARF MAGIC
Line One: 11, 2, 6
Line Two: 11, 13, 10
Line Three: 9, 15, 9
Line Four: 8, 17, 18
Line Five: 13, 11, 15
Line Six: 9, 12, 14

Line Seven: 12, 12, 10
Line Eight: 10,14, 6
Line Nine: 14, 8, 8
Line Ten: 16, 13, 5
Line Eleven: 8, 7, 8
Line Twelve: 10, 12, 7
Line Thirteen: 7, 9
Line Fourteen: 10, 11

Page 48–APPLE EQUATIONS
1. 50 cents **2.** 3 **3.** 80 cents
4. sister, 30 cents **5.** 18 **6.** 9 **7.** 11 **8.** 3
9. 8 **10.** 9 **11.** 15 **12.** 7

PAGE 50–THE POISONED FRUIT
orange, velvet bag; banana, box; peach, basket; grapes, paper bag

PAGE 51–THE MIXED-UP BEDS
Grumpy, 4th; Sneezy, 3rd; Dopey, 1st; Bashful, 6th; Happy, 7th, Doc, 5th; Sleepy, 2nd

PAGE 63–THE ROYAL PARTIES
Duke, green velvet; Earl, red taffeta; King, purple silk; Prince, blue velvet

PAGE 71–FISHING FOR ANSWERS
1. 16 **2.** 6 **3.** 5 **4.** 16 **5.** 14

PAGE 72–AHOY, MATES!
pearl necklace, sea coral; gold ring, oyster shell; silver comb, treasure chest; ivory brush, sunken ship

PAGE 73, THE DIVER'S DILEMMA
fish, beside the coral reef; electric eel, under a rock; manta ray, hiding in the sand; shark, on the surface of the water; octopus, in a sunken ship

PAGE 83–THE FRIENDS' FAVORITE FLOWERS
Mary, tulips; Joan, petunias, Marta, roses; Carol, carnations

PAGE 92–BEASTLY PROBLEMS
1. 26, 14, 16 **2.** 10, 12, 14, 16 **3.** 12, 7, 4
4. 20, 30, 20 **5.** 1, 6, 10, 4, 9 **Total:** 15
6. 12, 8, 10, 6, 10 **Total:** 27

PAGE 93–THE BEAST DINES TONIGHT
Monday, chicken; Tuesday, steak, Saturday, ham; Sunday, lamb chops